Welcome . . .

If you are reading this (which obviously you are!) you are probably a fairly new coach who needs a little support in developing their skills and confidence in running a client session, yes?

Well great news, you have come to the right place.

As a new coach I found one of my greatest challenges was remembering all the tools and techniques I'd learnt, particularly when I was engaged with a client. I thought to myself, 'wouldn't it be great to have a handy guide of the techniques and tools, a directory where I could easily flip to the technique or tool that I needed, in that moment'. Well this is that guide, I couldn't find one, so I wrote one.

'Necessity is the mother of invention"
anon

Chances are that you like me, are a coach because you want to help, to provide a truly inspirational and unique service for your clients that facilitates their growth, goal achievement and wellbeing.

I believe that great training, from a proven and ethical training provider, is key to developing our skills. Once we have this we are then on our own in conversation with our clients and that's the time this guide has been developed for, to make it easier for you to run a sessions and to improve the quality of the service you give to your clients.

Everything going on in the world right now has made it so much more important for us to be working smarter, really understanding the pressures and concerns our clients have in this time of change and uncertainty.

Using this guide will help you to avoid making mistakes when you are coaching, support you as you develop your skills and create a service which your clients want to recommend to others.

Be prepared, be flexible, be present, be authentic, and always be the best you that you can be

Ali x

The Coaches' Resource Directory

This Quick Reference Guide for new coaches enables you to easily access models, patterns and techniques to assist in your development and in structuring and delivering your coaching sessions.

The Contents page gives you the list of models & techniques contained in the guide, the situation or issue for which they are most appropriate, and on which page you can find each section in the document.

Note, it is an aide memoir, not a step by step how to run a session. Do not depend on it, you have the skills and information you need now, do you not? Just use it as a refresh and a guide when you need it, feel a bit stuck or are just practicing.

Contents

Who am I?

I am Ali Bagley, lead coach at **AliBagleyCoaching.co.uk**. I am an Association for Professional Coaching Certified Member, NLP practitioner, Hypnosis Practitioner and Timeline Coach.

I help people to overcome overwhelm, smash through barriers and develop awesome motivation to realise their full personal and professional potential.

I support coaches as a coach's coach, particularly new coaches who need support and want to develop their niche and mission statement.

I provide coaching for professionals seeking to move forward to success by overcoming obstacles, resolving conflict and developing a bespoke professional development plan

Coaches need coaches. We more than anyone know the value a coach brings to our lives.

For a free, no obligation discovery call with me please visit my website: **AliBagleyCoaching.co.uk**

or message me on LinkedIn:

https://www.linkedin.com/in/ali-bagley-apc-certified-life-coach-4b343721/

The Discovery Call

This is probably the most critical meeting you will have with your client. It will involve the key elements of:

1. Building initial rapport with your client
2. An opportunity for you both to decide whether you are the right coach for the client and that the client is happy to work with you.
3. It's an opportunity for you to explain how you work and what you can offer
4. It's the time when your client will outline what they want / need
5. If asked, you will outline your pricing structure, if not asked don't push it
6. Set a date / time for the first session
7. Set follow-up actions – send out *client agreement and *pricing structure, send your contact details, website address etc.

The meeting / call should last approximately 45 minutes. It is not a coaching call as such however it is very likely that some coaching will be involved in order for the client to understand how you can help them and appreciate the value that will bring to their life.

When discussing the clients' requirements focus on deep diving questions into their goal. You may need to run an appropriate NLP pattern (*see contents page*) to help them see the benefit of your service in relation to their needs. Check where they are now (reality check) and where they want to be – scale it, use the miracle question etc.

At the end of the call always agree the next steps.

When it comes to the price – it has to be discussed but only if the client asks. Begin the conversation by saying that you think you can work well together and outline the best package for the client (1 session, block booking etc.). State the price/s if the client asks, if they don't ask then a) they are either minted or b) not interested in booking with you.

If the client starts making excuses for why they can't book right now – need to think about it, not sure they can afford it, need to speak to partner about it etc. – this is where the *coaching comes in as you need to coach the client through their fear of not committing to something that they have already told you they want and you have both worked through and agreed how you can supply that service / outcome.

Book the first session with the client and let them know you will send them a zoom link (or whatever media you have agreed to use) for that session. When we can do face to face confirm the arrangements verbally and send confirmation of time, date address etc. after the call.

Tell them you will be sending a *client agreement for them to sign and return to you. Make sure they have your contact details and you have theirs.

*Templates for client agreements, session reports, pricing structure and coaching on overcoming client reticence are available as part of my one to one coaching service available through **AliBagleyCoaching.co.uk**

A Simple Coaching Structure – The GROW Model

This section is about the structure within which you might run your client sessions.

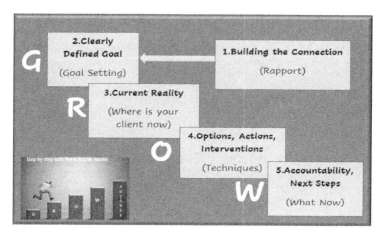

Step 1: You are looking to . . .

1. Build a connection with the person
    a. Notice: Changes in posture, Changes in facial expression, Shifts in skin colour/tonus, Changes in the shape of the mouth
    b. Mirror / Match Posture, Gestures, Facial expressions, Breathing, Words and phrases, Common interest/experiences. Do not mirror / match accents.
2. Create the coach/client contract – what you propose to do and what you expect from your client.
3. Establish the ground rules – ask permission to take notes / record the session etc.

4. Agree the structure – 'preframe' how the session will run and get acceptance from the client that they are happy to proceed.

Step 2: Clarify the 'Headline Goal'

1. Questions to ask to elicit the goal:
   a. What do you want?
   b. Why is it important to you?
   c. How will you know you are successful?
   d. Who do you become when you get it?
      i. What does that goal look like to you? *Visual*
      ii. What does your goal feel like to you? *Kinaesthetic*
      iii. What do you hear when you think about your goal? *Auditory*

Killer Questions: (Checks the ecology)

1. What will happen if you achieve your goal?
2. What will happen if you DON'T achieve your goal?
3. What WON'T happen if you achieve your goal?
4. What won't happen if you DON'T achieve it?

Step 3: Current Reality – The Reality Check

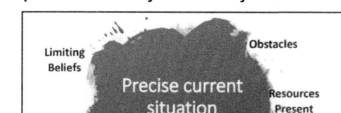

You have established your client's goal. Now is the time to check where your client is now in relation to that goal.

Questions to ask to gauge where the client is now:

1. What is stopping you from achieving your goal/s?
2. How do you feel right now when you think about your goal?
3. On a scale of 1 to 10, with 1 being never going to happen and 10 being I'm almost there already, how confident are you of achieving your goal?
4. What resources do you **need** to get it? *(knowledge, skills, support)*
5. What do you need to **do** to get it? *Attitude / Aptitude (mindset)*
6. What needs to change for you to reach your goal?
7. Where on the scale would you like to be by the end of this session? By the end of our time together?

The key is to identify what is holding them back, limiting beliefs, perceived obstacles, lack of resources. Once the client has identified their limits / obstacles etc. this will enable you to decide which techniques to use in Step 4 to help them more to their goal.

Step 4. Options, Actions, Interventions (Techniques and Models)

Create an experience for your client, unique to them, about them, for them, with them.

Based on your clients goal and what they need to do to achieve that goal you will run appropriate NLP / Hypnosis / Timeline techniques and/or deep dive questioning using the Milton Model (Chunking Up), the Meta Model (Chunking down) and framing / reframing.

Refer to the contents page to go to the information on the techniques and models.

Always remember when running any NLP pattern:

- R.R.R.O.E. (**R**esourceful coach. **R**apport. **R**esourceful client, **O**bjective/s. **E**cology check)
- Preframe
- Run the pattern
- Test it
- Future pace it

Step 5: Accountability, Next Steps, What next

Elicit actions to be taken

1. Agree and gain commitment on client actions – what they will do and when they will do it by
2. Agree realistic coaching support between sessions – be very clear on boundaries here
3. Set up accountability – when to check in with you to confirm they have carried out their commitments

4. Scaling at the beginning and end of the session (use linguistic presuppositions of success) i.e. *you stated at the beginning of our session that you were a (lets say 3) in confidence of achieving your goal and that by the end of the session you wanted to be a 6. How far beyond 6 are you now?*

Running a Values Assessment

It is very important that your clients' goals are aligned with their personal values system. If they are not then the client will probably never commit to the changes required to achieve their goal.

What is alignment in relation to coaching and values:

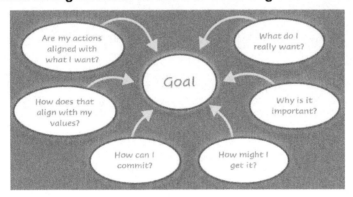

The Logical Levels (R Dilts)

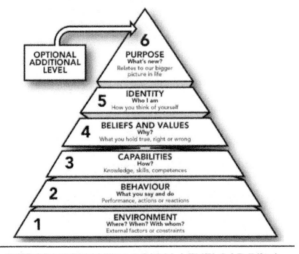

INTRODUCTION TO LOGICAL LEVELS (R.Dilts)

PURPOSE: What do you want? Who else would benefit...?

IDENTITY: Who do you need to be to get it? Who do you want to be?

BELIEFS & VALUES: Why is that important to you? Which value are you honouring? What value would that have to you?

CAPABILITIES: How can you get it? What skills do you need? What competencies will you develop?

BEHAVIOR: How will you get there? What are the most important actions? What kind actions you can start with?

ENVIRONNEMENT: When are you going to do it? Where will that happen?

A values assessment session needs to be run as either part of the first session or as the second session as it will create the foundation for aligning the client with their goals and help to reinforce their commitment to the process.

You will be taking the client through an exploration of their beliefs and values, to drill down to find out how the client is thinking, related to what they have told you they want, why they want it and what might be limiting them from getting it.
The exploration consists of questions designed to chunk down into the detail of the clients' value system (*see section on the Meta Model page 15*).

Use questions that look forward instead of backwards and focus on the positive.

Use these **miracle questions** as a starting point:
Imagine . . .

. . . you have everything you need, what would that change? What would you do?

. . . you already found your solution, how would you know? What would be possible now?

. . . you wake up tomorrow, and a miraculous change has happened whilst you slept. What would be different now? How would you know? What do you notice? How would other people notice a change in your behaviour?

- What would you see? (Visual)
- What would you hear? (Auditory)
- What would you feel? (Kinaesthetic)

. . . if you knew you couldn't fail, what would you do now? What would you really want? What actions could you take? What else? What would you do differently? Who else would notice?

Identifying your clients' values

- Every client has their own meaning attached to any value.
- Client's values represent their core truth, essence and uniqueness.
- Values tend to be summarised in one word: FREEDOM, LOVE, PEACE. . .
- Values are very personal. They have deep individual meanings for people.
- A clients journey becomes more meaningful when their values are aligned with their vision and goals.
- Values can be explicit or discovered through our actions and experience.

The main 4 themes of values are:

IDENTITY: Discovering, knowing, and confirming who you are.

STRENGTH: Having a feeling that what you do has an impact. Meaning of efficiency.

ACCOMPLISHMENT: Creating Awareness about fundamentals of growth for being fulfilled.

CONNECTION: Love and interdependence. Having a feeling of belonging to an individual or a group.

Here are some suggested value assessment / clarification questions to use during the client session. Notice the words and emotions your client displays as they answer the questions for clues as to what really matters to them.

- If you were watching your funeral, observing the goings on, what would you want people to say about you? What would you like them to be feeling? Why would that be important to you?
- If you were to receive an award at the end of your life? What would be the award for? What would you tell people?
- What is your favourite animal? What do you specifically love about them?
- Pick People (2 to 3) that you admire (well known or not, dead or not, people you know or haven't met....) What is it that you love/admire about them?
- What do you absolutely need in your life to feel accomplished and fulfilled? What kind of value do you need to honour in order to get that?
- If you were to be stuck in an island for a long period of time, and you can take 3 to 5 books/friends/movies... What would they be? What's so important about these books/friends/movies?
- Who are you at your best?
- What qualities do you look for in friendship? What's important about them?
- What if you could be a tree? What kind of tree? What's important about this tree?

- If you were at the end of your life, and you could talk to your kids, wife, friends, What would you want to tell them?
- Imagine you had great successful life: What are the 3 things most important that you have learned?
- What gives you the most joy, satisfaction and excitement? What's important about these 3....?
- What are the 10 most important thing in your life? WHY? Scale from 1 to 10.

Peak Moments in Time

1. Identify 3 special, peak moments when life was especially rewarding
2. What was important about this moment?
3. What values were you living in this moment?

What's most important to you?

1. What's most important today? This week? This month? This year?
2. What's important about the next five years? The next twenty years?
3. What's important about your life?

Must Haves

1. What (beyond basic needs) must have you in your life to be fulfilled?
2. What are the values you absolutely must honour - or part of you dies?

Suppressed Values

1. What are you willing to get into trouble to?
2. What value is being expressed here?
3. What gets you angry or frustrated?
4. What value is being violated?

Use whatever questions you feel are relevant to your client, that you feel comfortable with, as long as they help you to identify your clients' key values.

In conclusion, to cement the goal aligned to the clients' value system try the following:

Coach - What do you want? **Client** - I want A

Coach - When you have A, What will that really get for you? **Client** - I will have B

Coach - When you have B, What will you really get? **Client** - I will have C

Etc… repeat the process until the client can't find anything else

Coach - So the Value of A is… the final benefit that your client is able to drill down to

Example:

I want to lose weight. *When you lose weight, what will that really get for you?* I will feel good, confident. *When you feel confident, what will that really get for you?* I will feel comfortable and capable. *When you are comfortable…?* I will do more in my life. *When …What…….?* I will go after my dreams. *When…What…?* I will find a partner and feel I belong. *When…What…?* I will create a family, I would feel fulfilled. *What else?* That would already be amazing…

VALUE: If you lose weight, and you start to feel confident, and you go after your dreams, you start to create a family and start to be fulfilled and amazing you create the possibility of BELONGING ? Is that what you want? YES, that's exactly what I want

The Milton Model

Using 'Milton' language to 'Chunk Up' to the clients overarching issues / goals / requirements

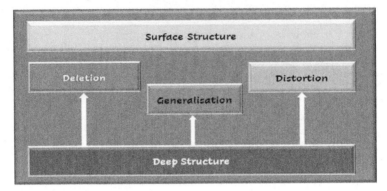

Uses:

1. Abstract language patterns

2. Works WITH the filters – distortion, deletion and generalization

3. Connects with the unconscious mind (trance)

17 key techniques:

1. Mind read – I know that, right now, you are thinking . . .
2. Lost performative – Breathing is good (who says so?)
3. Cause and effect – practice makes progress
4. Complex equivalence - Being late means you are not interested . . . (assumption)
5. Presuppositions - Will you sign the contract before or after we have coffee?
6. Universal quantifier - Everyone knows we need a better education system . . . (do they?)
7. Modal operators - I have to be there for my family . . .

8. Nominalisation - Close your eyes and consider your learnings so far . . .
9. Unspecified Verbs and Nouns – they really hurt me . . .
10. Lack of Referential Index – people can change
11. Comparative Deletion – this one is much better (than what?)
12. Tag questions - You'll find this easier with time, will you not?
13. Pace current experience - As you sit there, listening to my voice . . .
14. The double bind - Shall we do the exercise now or after the break? (similar to presuppositions)
15. Conversational Postulate – Can you lend me your pen . . . (response generated is not the answer to the question)
    And 15a - Extended Quote - A rambling context for the delivery of information or a hiddencommand. - I remember once speaking with Richard Bandler and he said
    to me, 'You are making deep changes now.
16. Utilisation - The sound of the passing traffic signifies the passing of time . . .
17. Ambiguity and Lack of Specificity – By and buy / t filling the freezers with the managers etc.

Example:

The NLP Communication Model

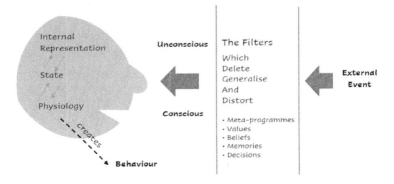

The Meta Model

The Art of asking the right question

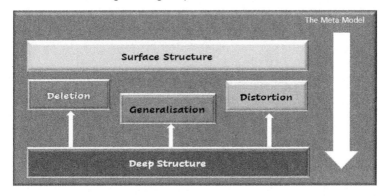

Chunking down into the deep structure

The key questions here are . . .

- WHO
- HOW
- WHAT
- WHERE
- WHEN

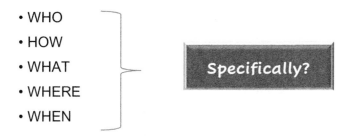

'WHY' will only give you a story or an excuse.

In asking the questions use softening patterns to maintains rapport and reduce the "interrogation" factor.

• "I'm wondering . . . "   • "That's interesting . . ."   •
"I'm curious . . . "

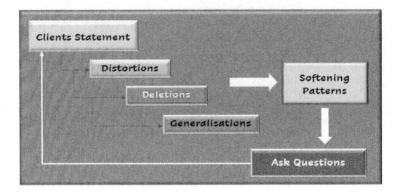

The Satir Funnel Game

Generalisation

Seven Words

Six Words

Five Words

Four Words

Three Words

Two Words

Specifics

Questioning and responding in ever decreasing words to get to the core of the matter:

Coach – asks question in seven words

Client – responds to the question in seven words

Coach – asks another question in relation to the clients seven-word response, in six words

Client - responds in six words

Client - asks another question in relation to the clients six-word response, in five words

Client – responds in five words

And so on until you get to the core of the matter . . .

Framing and Reframing

The art of looking at a negative statement and turning around into a positive statement.

'Frame' – the meaning that we attach to an experience

'Reframe' – changing the content or the context in order to bring a more useful meaning to the experience

'These NLP exercises are really challenging' to 'I am learning so much from these NLP exercises'

'I don't think my boss trusts me; he's always sending me on courses!' to 'my boss must really value me as he is investing in my development'

In coaching, when a client makes a negative statement, ask them to reframe it to a positive (or reframe it for them if they struggle).

The Sub-modalities Checklist

A very useful tool for turning a like into a dislike and a dislike into a like.

Key uses:

Like to dislike i.e.

Food/drink – turn your client off a food/drink they can't resist (chocolate, wine, cheese, pizza, beer etc.) by replacing the sub-modalities of that choice with the sub-modalities of a food/drink they don't like.

Dislike to like i.e.

Activity – turn your client to an activity they can't get motivated to do (exercise, write that book, plan their next career move) by replacing the sub-modalities of that activity with the sub-modalities of an activity they really enjoy

Using the Sub-modalities Checklist:

The process: to turn a like to a dislike

1. R.R.R.O.E.
2. Preframe
3. Run the pattern

Ask the client to get a picture of the food / drink they like in their minds eye.

Run through all of the questions on the sub-modalities checklist, without stopping to overthink responses, and note the clients responses in column one.

Break the state – ask about the weather, what they plan for the weekend etc.

Not ask the client to picture the food / drink they don't like in their minds eye.

Sub-Modalities Checklist

Make a picture	1	2	3	4
Visual				
Black/ White or Colour				
Near or Far				
Bright or Dim				
Location				
Size of Picture				
Associated or Dissociated				
Focused or Defocused?				
Framed or Panoramic?				
Movie or Still?				
Movie-Fast/Normal/Slow				
Amount of Contrast				
3D or Flat				
Angle Viewed From				

Auditory — Are there any sounds that are important?				
Location				
Direction				
Internal or External?				
Loud or Soft?				
Fast or Slow?				
High or Low? (Pitch)				
Tonality				
Timbre				
Pauses				
Tempo				
Duration				
Uniqueness of Sound				

Kinaesthetic — Are there any feelings that are important?				
Location				
Size				
Shape				
Intensity				
Steady or changing				
Temperature hot/cold				
Vibration				
Pressure/Heat?				
Weight				

Are there any smells or tastes that are important?	Speed is very important.	Look for the trigger.

Run through all of the questions on the sub-modalities checklist, without stopping to overthink responses, and note the clients responses in column two.

Break the state.

Mark all of the responses that are different between column one and column two. Ignore all of the responses that are the same. (Mapping across)

Ask the client to picture the food / drink they like again.

Using the responses in column 2 that are different to those in column one ask the client to change the picture, sounds and feelings associated with that picture. For instance:

Differences noted from the exercise			
Element	Column 1	Column 2	Change the picture
Black / white Colour	Black white	colour	Change picture from B&W to colour
Bright / Dim	Bright	dim	Change picture from bright to dim
Location	In front	To the right	Move picture to the right
Size	Big	small	Shrink the picture down to small
Moving or still	Still	moving	Make the picture move
Sound loud or soft	Loud	soft	Change the sound to soft
Tone high or low	Low	High	Lift the pitch to high
Location of feeling	In my stomach	In my throat	Move the feeling into your throat
Shape of feeling	round	square	Change the shape of the feeling to a square
Size of feeling	big	small	Shrink the feeling down to small

4. Break the state
5. Test it - ask the client to picture the food / drink they like again. Do they want it now?
6. Future pace it

Reverse the exercise to turn a dislike into a like.

The Swish Pattern

Used to replace a negative / unhelpful state / behaviour by replacing it with a positive potential new reality.

It is a High-speed, sub-modalities change (the Habit Buster). Works better if client is sitting.

The Process

1. R.R.R.O.E.
2. Identify un-useful state and 'trigger' – creates a picture
3. Client Associates fully into undesired state – moves into the picture of themselves in that state big, bold, clear and puts that image in front of themselves (places right hand in front as if looking at the picture.
4. Client Creates a diss-associated image of themselves, their ideal future self, in the desired state – they are looking in at it.
5. Client Shrinks desired image down to pinpoint, fuzzy, and moves it to their left knee – placing left hand, palm up, on their knee.
6. Client Closes their eyes and 'Swish" up the pinpoint image, making it clear and bright and bold, to replace undesired state – left hand raises pinpoint picture as right hand throws out to the right. They shout SWISH as they do this.
7. Repeat steps 5 and 6 faster and faster
8. Stop when fully associated into desired state
9. Break state and test

Anchoring Useful States

Anchoring works by connecting a specific stimulus (anchor) to a specific state.

Anchors occur across all modalities

- Visual anchors
- Auditory anchors
- Kinaesthetic anchors
- Olfactory anchors
- Gustatory anchors
- Even spatial anchors
- AND – multiple modalities

Five Keys to success . . .

1. Intensity of the experience
2. Timing
3. Uniqueness of state
4. Ease of replication
5. Repetition

Creating a simple Kinaesthetic Anchor

The process . . .

1. R.R.R.O.E.
2. Identify desired state and location for anchor – knuckle, elbow etc.
3. Elicit state and calibrate for physiological changes – client remembers or imagines when they were fully in this state (confident, calm, happy, fearless etc.). Make the image clear, bright, see what they see, hear what they hear, feel what they feel.
4. Break state
5. Repeat steps 3 and 4 at least twice – remember the break state
6. Elicit state and anchor at peak – at the point where the client is fully emersed in the state they need to press on their anchor point for about 10 seconds
7. Break state
8. Test – press anchor point, what do they see, feel, etc.

Stacking Resource Anchors

This technique is used to stack individual DIFFERENT resource anchors.

The states must be 'complimentary', i.e. confident, calm and successful.

Client utilises the same stimulus point, all the states anchored in one point.

The Process

1. R.R.R.O.E.
2. Identify desired states and location for anchor – knuckle, elbow etc.
3. Elicit state and calibrate for physiological changes – client remembers or imagines a time when they were fully in this state (confident, calm, happy, fearless etc.). Make the image clear, bright, see what they see, hear what they hear, feel what they feel.
4. Break state
5. Repeat steps 3 and 4 at least twice – remember the break state
6. Elicit state and anchor at peak – at the point where the client is fully emersed in the state they need to press on their anchor point for about 10 seconds
7. Break state
1. Repeat steps 2 to 7 for each required state
8. Test – press anchor point, what do they see, feel, etc.

Shifting Perceptual Positions

When your client needs to step out of themselves and view their issue, challenge, behaviour and needs from different points of view.

It works well in:

- Relationships – personal AND business
- Relationship with self
- Rehearsing for a meeting/presentation
- Training
- Conflict management

The Mercedes Model

The Perspectives

1st Position
Self

Associated and seeing the world through own eyes

2nd Position
Other

Seeing the world through their eyes

3rd Position
Observer

Objective and impartial (Fly on the wall)

Running the process

1. R.R.R.O.E.
2. Client identifies the issue
3. Client puts themselves into 1st Position – what do they see, feel, hear
4. Move through the three positions
5. Client gains perspective at 2nd Position – Client describes how does the other person sees things
6. Client gains insights and advice at 3rd Position – acting as an observer what does the client have to say about both position 1 and position 2 perspectives, what advice would they give.
7. Finish at 1st Position and calibrate for change – what does the client think now, see now, feel now.
8. Repeat process as required

The Disney Strategy (or the Creative Strategy)

Similar to the Shifting Perceptual Positions technique, this technique is particularly useful in business coaching when a business owner or decision maker needs to examine the possibilities of changes in their business. The Disney Strategy involves the client seeing their issue or situation from 3 perspectives:

Position 1: The Dreamer (the vision maker who sees all the possibilities). Thinks about who they will become, why it's important? Who else benefits? They step into the dream and experience it. As they experience that dream, they let you know how they feel.

Position 2: The Realist (the Do-er, the executor and organiser). They think about how this can be implemented? What resources do we need? How can we get what we want? What are the next steps?

Position 3: The Wise Critic (the evaluator, the disassociated inner voice, sees from a negative or neutral standpoint). What can stop you with this project? What additional things needs to be considered? What else can possibly stop you?

Running The Process

1. R.R.R.O.E.
2. Client identifies the issue
3. Client puts themselves into 1st Position – they talk about the detail of what they think they should do to improve the situation or issue, why it's important to them, the benefits. Get them to step into the dream of the possibilities.
4. Client then moves to second position
5. Client gains perspective at 2nd Position – Client questions the dream - how can this be

implemented? What resources do we need? How can we get what we want? What are the next steps?

6.   Client moves back and forth between the dreamer and the realist, discussing the situation.
7.   Client moves to 3rd position, the wise critic.
8.   Client gains insights and advice at 3rd Position – the client now thinks about the situation questioning - What can stop you with this project? What additional things needs to be considered? What else can possibly stop you?
9.   The client steps back to position 2 (the realist) to discuss the situation with position 3, the wise critic.
10.   NB: THE CRITIC NEVER TALKS TO THE DREAMER
11.   END THE CLIENT ON DREAMER, seeing the dream as fixed and committing to it.
12.   Then the client steps back to COACH POSITION and discusses the experience – what does the client think now, see now, feel now.
13.   What did you learn? What's possible? How can you commit yourself? What's your next steps? Action plan.

Using a Future Pace

To lock in changes the client has made as a result of an NLP pattern.

Remember to check the ecology of any negative consequences of locking in this new behaviour before you start.

The Keys to a great future pace are:

- Load your language with Milton
- Take them into the future
- Anchors – Vi Au & Ki
- Linguistic presupposition to finish

Here is an example of a future pace that is loaded with Milton language and is perfect for embedding a new behaviour after you have run a pattern:

I'd like you to just close your eyes, and as you sit now, listening to my voice, I want you to think about this.

We are going to take a journey into the future. In a little while from now, not yet, in a little while from now, I will ask you to open your eyes. When you do so, as you open your eyes, you will be looking at the world through the eyes of someone who, has a new behaviour now. Do you not?

And a little later in time, after our conversation has finished, you will probably have a conversation with someone else, Whoever that is, wherever that is, the moment that you hear them speak, that will be the reminder that you need , that you have an you behaviour now, do you not?

Finally, at the end of the day, as you relax, ready to sleep, just as you are relaxing now, as you relax ready to sleep, you do so in the knowledge that you have a new behaviour now. Do you not?

So, when you accept all of that, and only when you accept all of that, you can open your eyes now, thank you

(Credit to Ralph 'The White Wolf' Watson for permission to use this script)

Solution Focused Coaching

Similar to the GROW model but focused on creating a solution for the client in a less formal way, with deep questioning.

The Principles of Solution Focused Coaching:

Developed from solution-focused brief therapy

- The coach will work with the person and not the problem
- Concentrates on the resources and not the deficits
- Explores the options for preferred and possible futures
- Explores what is already contributing to those possible futures
- Treats the client as the 'expert' in all aspects of their own lives

The process involves problem-free talk and is based on outcomes and 'best hopes' for the session or programme.

Scaling

This is a useful tool used in solution focused coaching for scaling either the problem or the motivational level. It works on a zero to ten scale where zero is no problem or no motivation and ten is catastrophic problem or massive motivation.

Use it initially to scale the current state, ask the client to set the desired scale at the end of the session and then scale again at the end of the session to check the outcome. Tip – if client stated they wanted a six by the end of the session then phrase your question as:

'So, you scaled your motivation/problem as a three at the beginning of the session and said you wanted to achieve a six. Tell me, _where above six are you now_ on the scale?'

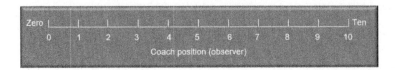

The Miracle Question

During the session, when establishing the goal, the miracle question is a fantastic tool for implanting the possibility of a new reality in the client.

How does this work? . . .

1. Connects client with the 'existence of solution'

2. Presupposition that, because they know the problem, they must have the contrast frame

3. Begins to build a multi-sensory experience of the preferred reality

4. Often highlights what needs to change

5. Opens the client up to possibilities and opportunities

It goes something like this:

'Imagine that tonight, while you are asleep, a miracle happens and when you wake up your hopes have been realised and your goal successfully achieved, but because you were asleep you didn't realise this miracle had happened. What are you going to notice that's different when you awake that begins to tell you that this miracle has happened?'

What will be the . . .

- First thing you see?
- First thing you hear?
- First thing you feel in yourself?
- What will you be doing differently?
- What will you see others doing?
- What will you be hearing others saying?

During a solutions focused coaching session remember these things:

- Maintain focus on the desired reality
- Run appropriate NLP interventions
- Agree and gain commitment on client actions
- Agree realistic coaching support between sessions
- Set up accountability
- Scaling at the beginning and end of the session (use linguistic presuppositions of success)

Coaching with Timeline

Timeline coaching is based on using the 'temporal' and 'spatial' submodalities. All of our experiences are 'encoded' in our unconscious mind and our UNCONSCIOUS mind can find those, even if our conscious mind can't. Bear in mind that in our clients mind, some events may have been shielded to 'protect' them.

Primarily we use Timeline to release and deal with negative emotions. Our role as coach is to facilitate the client in releasing negative emotion stemming from a single 'root-cause' event or chain of events; a negative emotion that may be preventing them from achieving their desired goals.

Negative emotions can include, but are not limited to:

Fear   **Anger**   **Lack of**   **Shame**   **Grief**   **Regret**
                             self-love

The Process

1. R.R.R.O.E.
2. Preframe
3. Identify un-useful emotion – root cause or trigger event (if the client struggles to find the root cause or trigger event ask them to ask their subconscious mind to guide them to it, then relax and wait for it to come)
4. Elicit Timeline – useful to explain to client to imagine timeline is behind them for the past and in front for the future.

5. Start at now, float up and back, stopping above the event
6. Observe, take useful learnings and store them. Ask if client wants to share what they see and what they are learning.
7. Float to short time BEFORE the event and float DOWN, say to client - notice the emotion has 'gone now' (Milton embedded command)
8. Float forward SUCCESSFULLY through the event, taking useful learnings
9. Move forward to now, noticing how all other similar events are changed
10. Stop at now
11. Test by thinking back to that event – the client should now be able to see that event differently, in a way that the un-useful emotion has gone now.
12. Future pace to bed it in

'As you sit there now, listening to my voice and hearing my words, you know that you have a new understanding now. The human brain is a wonderful thing, is it not? To think that just listening to my voice now means that you are already learning, and that learning will lead to more understanding. You understand now, where that un-helpful emotion was coming from, that you do not need it now, that you have a new pattern now, do you not? That makes sense, doesn't it?'

Using Timeline to deal with anxiety about a forthcoming event

As with the previous exercise you will be taking your client to a future point, needs to be specific, in order to help them to face that point in time without unhelpful anxiety.

The Process

1. R.R.R.O.E.
2. Preframe
3. Elicit timeline (or work 'as if') – working in front for a future event
4. Start at 'now'
5. Consider forthcoming event – specific date, specific event, and notice the emotions
6. Float above timeline and forward to above the event
7. Observe and take learnings
8. Move forward, float down and look back at event – notice change and learnings
9. Bring all learnings, float up, back to now and float back down
10. Test by thinking forward to the event and noticing what's changed

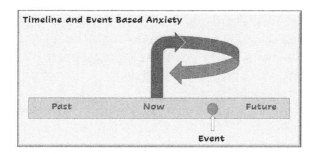

Timeline and Event Based Anxiety

Past   Now   Future

Event

Timeline and a compelling goal

This is a combination of:

- Timeline
- Well-formed outcome
- Perceptual positions
- Resource anchor (spatial)

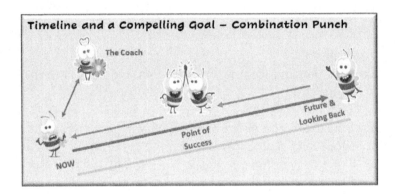

The Combination Punch (copyright Ralph Watson)

The process . . .

1. R.R.R.O.E.
2. Preframe
3. Start at 'NOW' – elicit outcome and check for well formedness
4. Pinpoint 'moment of success'
5. Make action plan to get to the point of success
6. Move out to 'COACH' position (3rd perceptual position*) – observe, revise action plan, advice and learning
7. Return to 'NOW' and update action plan and timing if necessary

8. Move into 'FUTURE' ('having successfully achieved outcome') and stop 'LATER IN LIFE'
9. Look back on life and note the positive benefits and learnings because of success
10. Move to 'MOMENT OF SUCCESS' – get full VAK association and anchor on Timeline
11. Return to 'NOW' – integrate learnings, scale motivation and get action commitment

Hypnosis Techniques

Before any hypnosis technique always carry out R.R.R.O.E – ethics are key

Suggestibility testing . . .

- Relaxes the client
- Introduces the concept of 'trance'
- Begins educating the mind

The Lemon

> **The Lemon**
>
> Sit back and relax and close your eyes.
>
> It's a very warm day and you are really thirsty, feel your mouth getting dry now.
>
> Get up and go into the kitchen, open the fridge. In the fridge is a bottle of ice-cold water and a juicy lemon.
>
> Pour the water into a glass, slice the juicy lemon and drop a slice into the ice-cold glass of water.
>
> Now, raise the glass to your lips . . .

If client is willing to accept the hypnosis he should now be salivating at the thought of the drink.

Dictionary and Balloon

> **The Dictionary and the Balloon**
>
> Sit back and relax and close your eyes.
>
> Put your hands out in front of you, lovely. Now turn the palm of your right hand up to face the ceiling. Great.
>
> You can imagine, can you not, a ribbon is tied to the middle finger of your left hand, and attached to the ribbon is a big, red, helium filled balloon that gently lifts your hand upwards.
>
> Now, imagine that I have placed two heavy books into the palm of your right hand. Feel the weight of the books as they press your hand lower . . .

If client is willing to accept the hypnosis his left hand will be up, and his right hand will have gone down. Your client must agree to, and be willing to, accept hypnosis. If he does not, then none of the following techniques will work.

The Hypnosis Process . . .

1. Pre-trance talk (pre-frame)

2. **Always** get clients agreement to take part in the process

3. Initial induction

4. Deepening trance (where required)

5. Script work

6. Post hypnotic suggestion (future pace)

7. Bring out / Grounding / 8. Hypnosis is a learning state

A technique for a Progressive relaxation induction

Close your eyes now, relax the tiny muscles around your eyes now

Really relax those muscles, and test that your eyes are closed and relaxed by moving eyebrows up and down

Keep eyes closed and let a huge wave of relaxation go from the top of your head right down to the soles of your feet

In a moment, not yet, I will ask you to open your eyes. When you do, close them again straight away and double down that relaxation to the soles of your feet

Open your eyes, close your eyes, double that relaxation all the way down

Make it happen, want it to happen and it will happen

Open your eyes, close your eyes, double that relaxation again, all the way down

Wrap yourself in a warm blanket of relaxation, open your eyes, close your eyes, double that relaxation again, all the way down

Repeat steps 6 and 7 three more times, doubling the relaxation each time, deeper and deeper

Test. In the room, lift the client's hand and tell them that when you let go, they let it drop like a wet cloth. Online – ask client to imagine they cannot lift their right hand as it's tied down, ask them to try to lift it – if they can then they are not in trance.

Ask the client to begin counting back from 100. Tell them that after a few numbers all the numbers will disappear

You can mentally relax by counting back from 100 now, Client - 100, deep relax, 99 deep relax, 98 deep relax . . .

Drop the numbers, just push them out of your mind, all gone?

Make sure client says yes or nods to be sure the numbers have gone

Client is now in deep trance / relaxation and ready for suggestion.

When ready, ask your client to come back, only when they are ready and have learnt their new behaviour, attitude etc., gently coming back up into the now at their own pace.

And come back.

Progressive relaxation induction is simple and doesn't take very long. Excellent for initial trance experiences. Progress physical relaxation from head to toes. Induces mental relaxation. From the David Elman Induction Technique

Keys to success

- Rapport
- Pace and lead the client's breathing with your voice
- Voice tonality
- Language

The 'Secret Place' . . .

A simple and very useful hypnotic intervention

- The unconscious mind works in metaphor
- The 'secret place' is a metaphor FOR the unconscious mind
- Can be used to gather 'resources'
- Can be used to integrate change, learnings etc.

You are standing on a street corner opposite a ten-story office building.

Its twilight on a Friday evening, all the lights are on in the building, the office workers are ready to go home and, relax now.

As you stand looking at the building you start to see the lights going off on each floor.

Floor ten, the lights go off, Moving down deeper, floor 9, the lights go off, Deeper still, floor 8, the lights turn off.

Down again and the lights go off on floor seven, now six, and off on 5.

All the way down to floor 4 now and the lights go off, floor three now, and down nearly all the way to floor two and the lights go off.

Now at floor 1, the last lights turn off and you find yourself on the bottom floor.

Here in this deep, relaxing secret place, you see a door. Imagine the door, the colour, the size, the texture.

This door leads to a place only you can go, a secret place where all of your memories, experiences and learnings are stored, ready for you to retrieve them whenever you need them.

Only you have the key to this wonderful secret place. Take the key and open the door now. Walk into your secret place, see what you see, feel what you feel, hear what you hear.

And now ask for what you need (it might be confidence, wisdom, calmness, a memory your client needs to access etc.)

Take what you need from the room and bring it with you, back to now. Close the door and as I count from 1 to five, gradually come back to now with your new learnings. 1, 2, 3, 4, open eyes 5.

Remember, you can go back here anytime by just relaxing and counting down from 10.

Remember to make it 'safe' and 'secret'

Hypnosis for fears and phobias

The double dissociation phobia cure

1. R.R.R.O.E.
2. Identify the 'fear' and scale it (1 to 10 with 1 being no fear to 10 being I will die if faced with this) as a coach, not a therapist, do not attempt to deal with any fear scaled above 5 as a max)
3. Preframe – explain what is going to happen for the client

The Double Dissociation Phobia Cure

Client relax and close their eyes

Imagine you are at the cinema, you are the only person there and once you have got your drink and your snack, find your way to a nice comfy seat in the center of the auditorium, and sit down.

In front of you, on the screen is a full colour movie. It goes like this:

You see someone on the screen, walking down the street and as they turn the corner, there in front of them is (*insert the persons fear i.e. spider, snake, pigeon etc.*). The movie ends.

The movie starts again, the same movie, You see someone on the screen, walking down the street and as they turn the corner, there in front of them is (insert the persons fear i.e. spider, snake, pigeon etc.). The movie ends.

Client watches this movie again, up to five or six times.

Now, you move from your seat up to the projection booth, here you are inside a thick Perspex bubble, very safe, nothing can get in but you can get out whenever you want to. You look down and you can see yourself watching the movie from your seat in the auditorium, the movie begins, you watch yourself, watching someone on the screen, walking down the street and as you turn the corner, there in front of them is (insert the persons fear i.e. spider, snake, pigeon etc.). The movie ends.

Now the movie rewinds at double speed, in black and white, back to the start. You watch yourself watching the movie again, this time at double speed, still in colour, then rewind at double double speed in black and white.

* repeat several times getting faster each time and adding funny music, (Benny Hill theme, keystone cops etc.)

Stop and break state.

Go back to your seat in the auditorium, watch the movie again, at normal speed, in colour, and this time watch it past where the person turns the corner and meets (insert clients fear).

Now ask the client to step into the movie, live it, walk down the street, turn the corner, come face to face with their fear, and move past it / through it/ kill it etc.

Hypnosis – The Betty Erickson Sleep System

This technique is used to relax your client but can also be taught to your client, so that they can use it on themselves when they need it outside of the session.

The process
1. R.R.R.O.E.
2. Preframe – explain what is going to happen for the client, as ever it is vital to get the clients agreement to the process. It is useful to explain to the client that when you ask them to create an image in their mind that the image needs to be fairly still and be of a safe, relaxing place.
3. Ask your client to relax, keep their eyes open and their body still and you then go through the script given below.

Script

Now, as you sit there, relaxing, listening to the sound of my voice, I want you to focus your attention on three things that you can see in front of you. Once you've got that just nod your head. Good, very good.

Now at the same time as you are focusing on the three things you can see I want you to become aware of three things that you can hear, and you may need to . . . listen carefully.

When you've got three things you can see and three things you can hear, and you are relaxing more, just nod your head. Very good.

Now I want you to become aware, to focus on those three things you can see and those three things you can hear, and I want you to become aware of three sensations, three things you can actually feel. When you've got all of that and you're relaxed even more, just nod your head, very good.

Now I want you to focus on two things you can see, on two things you can hear, and on two things you can feel. And at the same time as you're focusing on the two things you can see, the two things you can hear and the two things you can feel, I want you to create a pleasant image in your mind, and focus on one element of that image, it can be anything you choose, and one sound that goes with that image, focusing, and one sensation that goes with that image.

Remember to keep focusing on those two things out there, those two sounds out there and those two sensations out there, while you focus on the image, the sound, and the sensation inside your mind. Very good.

Now as you listen to my voice I want you to allow yourself now to just focus on one external thing, one thing that you can see, I want you to just focus on that one thing you can see out there, One sound that you can hear out there, one sensation that you can feel out there. While you focus on two elements of that pleasant image in your mind. And two sounds that go with that image, and two sensations that go with that image. Very good.

Now as you close your eyes completely, Let go of what you can see, hear and feel out there, as you focus on three elements of that image that you can see in your mind, focus, focus, focus. Focus on three sounds that go with that image in your mind, very good, and focus on three sensations that go with that image and that sound.

As I count down gently 5 4 3 2 1 Just relax, very good. So, in a moment I am going to count to 5 very quickly and when I reach 5 you will be wide awake and you will be ready to do this for yourself anytime you like. Ready, here we go 1, 2, 3, 4, and 5 (voice increases in pace and volume as you count). Good excellent open your eyes give yourself a shake. Check how the client is feeling now.

In Conclusion

I hope that this guide has been useful for you. It will never replace quality training, such as that offered by SPEAKUp and the incomparable Mr Ralph (The White Wolf) Watson.

As a disclaimer, please do not try this at home, and never on clients, unless and until you have the training and knowledge necessary to give your client a comprehensive service, with integrity, love and a genuine intention to help and support.

For more information, details on my one to one coaching and courses and to leave any feedback on this book please message me either through my Website, or my LinkedIn page.

Thank you and wishing you every success in your business,

Ali

Acknowledgements

I must thank 3 very important people without whom this guide would never have been written and without whom I would not be the coach that I am today:

Ralph 'the White Wolf' Watson. You are without doubt one of the most inspirational and supportive people I have ever met in my life. Your generosity and willingness to share your experience, skills and insights have changed my life. I could not recommend you more highly to anyone considering becoming a coach or anyone needing a coach.

Eric Bensoussan. Thank you for your teaching and your wonderful Frenchness (and weird sense of humour). My Thursday evenings will not be the same without you. You have a wonderful spirit and again I would recommend you without hesitation.

And **Bernie**, my rock, my number one fan. Thank you for your support, your belief and your sacrifices. I love you.

Printed in Great Britain
by Amazon